Extreme Biology

Kill or Die
Extreme Life Cycles

Louise Spilsbury

Gareth Stevens
PUBLISHING

Please visit our website, **www.garethstevens.com**. For a free color catalog of all our high-quality books, call toll free 1-800-542-2595 or fax 1-877-542-2596.

Library of Congress Cataloging-in-Publication Data

Spilsbury, Louise, author.
  Kill or die : extreme life cycles / Louise Spilsbury.
      pages cm. — (Extreme biology)
  Includes bibliographical references and index.
ISBN 978-1-4824-2248-1 (pbk.)
ISBN 978-1-4824-2249-8 (6 pack)
ISBN 978-1-4824-2246-7 (library binding)
1. Animal behavior—Juvenile literature. 2. Animal life cycles—Juvenile literature.
3. Animals—Adaptation—Juvenile literature. 4. Adaptation (Biology)—Juvenile literature.
I. Title.
 QL751.5.S67 2015
 591.56—dc23

                                    2014027567

First Edition

Published in 2015 by
Gareth Stevens Publishing
111 East 14th Street, Suite 349
New York, NY 10003

© 2015 Gareth Stevens Publishing

Produced by: Calcium, www.calciumcreative.co.uk
Designed by: Paul Myerscough
Edited by: Sarah Eason and John Andrews
Picture research by: Rachel Blount

Photo credits: Cover: Shutterstock: Trevor Kelly; Inside: Dreamstime: Andreanita 43, Creativenature1 17, DiversityStudio1 21, Joan Egert 42, Stephen Gibson 4, Hotshotsworldwide 40, Teh Soon Huat 8, Dmitry Knorre 14, Sekarb 28, Nico Smit 39, Olga N. Vasik 29; Shutterstock: BMJ 37, Aynia Brennan 18, Cbpix 22, Clearviewstock 5, Matt Cole 16, Creativemarc 24, T. Dallas 7, Erni 35, Evelyng23 31, David Evison 32, Stanislav Fosenbauer 36, Juan Gaertner 3, 12, 13, Eric Gevaert 44, Huxiaohua 25, Denise Kappa 6, Tan Kian Khoon 26, Heiko Kiera 30, 33, D. Kucharski K. Kucharska 11, Henrik Larsson 9, 19, Francesco de Marco 34, Mr Fiza 15, Optionm 23, Peter Vrabel 45, Worakit Sirijinda 41, Kitti Sukhonthanit 1, 20, Miro Vrlik Photography 27, Wild At Art 38; Wikimedia Commons: Gilles San Martin 10.

All rights reserved. No part of this book may be reproduced in any form without permission from the publisher, except by reviewer.

Printed in the United States of America

CPSIA compliance information: Batch #CW15GS: For further information contact Gareth Stevens, New York, New York at 1-800-542-2595.

Contents

Chapter 1 Super Survivors — 4

Chapter 2 Hitching a Ride — 10

Chapter 3 Creepy Crawly Tactics — 16

Chapter 4 Smart and Deadly Swimmers — 22

Chapter 5 Battles for Life — 30

Chapter 6 Killers and Caretakers — 38

Chapter 7 Completing the Life Cycle — 44

Glossary — 46
For More Information — 47
Index — 48

Chapter 1
Super Survivors

You and every other living thing on Earth are part of a life cycle. This is the journey from emerging as a new organism, through the stages of growth and development, to becoming an adult that can reproduce new organisms of the same type. The journey is full of big challenges, and some organisms use extreme tactics to make sure their life cycles succeed.

Circle of Life

Many animals start life as fertilized eggs that hatch into babies, which must become adults before they can reproduce. Most plants start life as seeds. Only if it has the right conditions, such as water, warmth, and light, can a seed start to develop into a young plant and ultimately grow big enough to produce its own seeds.

Banksia can regrow only after being burned. The burning dries out the cones enough for tiny slits to form that let out seeds.

Banksia Burnout

Banksia is an Australian shrub, and its extreme life cycle depends on fire. The plant makes its seeds in tough cases that look a bit like cones. For years these cases stay tightly closed to protect their seeds from animals, only opening to release the seeds after a brush fire. Then the seeds fall onto ground cleared of other plants and rich with nutrients from plant ash— good conditions for starting a new life cycle.

Banksia flower spikes contain lots of nectar that birds, bats, and other animals feed on.

Extreme!

Banksia Bombs!

Banksia cones can explode like bombs if they get hot enough. Firefighters in Australia use the cones to start small, controlled brush fires. They light the cones and throw them into the bush, where their explosions can set plants ablaze all around them. Burning like this can stop big brush fires from spreading and reaching homes.

Titan Arum

About once every three years, the rain forests of Indonesia witness a remarkable event—the flowering of the gigantic titan arum. This amazing plant produces the biggest and one of the smelliest flowers on Earth.

Flesh Flower

The titan arum looks like no other plant. It has a pale central spike, or spadix, up to 10 feet (3 m) high, surrounded by a purple frill 3 feet (1 m) across. The job of the towering spadix is to create an appalling smell, kind of like rotting fish flesh. This attracts lots of insects. They crawl down inside the base of the plant, expecting to find some juicy food but instead discover many miniflowers, which they pollinate with pollen picked up from other titan arums they have visited.

A titan arum spadix heats up to help spread its scent.

Fruit Tower

After the titan arum's flowers are pollinated, the frill collapses over the base of the spadix. The flowers change into bright red fruit and then the frill rots away. Forest animals such as hornbill birds feed on the berries and spread the seeds that were in the fruit in their waste. Finally the flower collapses. For the next two years, the only part of the arum to sprout from the ground is its leaves, which can soar to heights of more than 20 feet (6 m).

The giant leaves of the titan arum grow from a huge plant part called a tuber that lies under the soil.

Extra Extreme

The flower of the titan arum is not the only enormous thing about it. The flower and leaves grow from a huge underground stem called a tuber. This can weigh 150 pounds (68 kg) or more, which is as heavy as the average adult man.

Zombie Ant Fungus

On the damp floor of some forests, a tiny killer lurks waiting for a passing carpenter ant. This is a cordyceps fungus, also known as "zombie ant" fungus. The fungus gets its name because it turns the ant into a sort of zombie that it can control, in order to complete its life cycle.

Fungal Foe

Zombie ant fungus, like other fungi, makes spores rather than seeds. These tiny grains can grow into new individuals. As ants move across the forest floor collecting food to take back to their tree nests, spores from the fungus stick to them and break through their tough outer skin. The spores do this by building up as much pressure as there is inside a jumbo-jet tire and blasting a tiny hole in the ant. The spores then move in.

The mushroom hat of cordyceps bursts out of the carpenter ant's head. It can only produce spores once it has reached this stage.

Carpenter ants spend most of their lives up trees in group nests. Only the unfortunate ones on the forest floor get infested.

Mushroom Head

The fungal spores produce fungal threads that spread through and take over the ant's body. Meanwhile, chemicals released by the fungus change the way the ant behaves. They make it stumble around and finally climb up the stem of a plant. The ant locks its jaws onto the underside of a leaf, where it dies. Soon after, a mushroom grows out of the ant's head. The mushroom then drops its own spores onto the forest floor, and the life cycle is completed.

Extra Extreme

There are different cordyceps fungi that infect different species of insects—and one is worth a lot of money. The caterpillar fungus has been highly prized in Asia for centuries as a traditional medicine for treating anything from fatigue to cancer. It is collected from mountain pastures and sells for well over $5,000 a pound.

Chapter 2
Hitching a Ride

Parasites are living things that survive on or in other living things. They do not just hitch a ride but also steal from their hosts, usually by taking food. In the process, parasites often harm or make life difficult for their hosts.

Home Sweet Home

Many parasites, such as head lice, live from birth to death in or on one type of organism. Adult head lice live on human hair, where they feed on blood from the scalp and reproduce. Their eggs, known as nits, hatch into baby head lice, leaving behind tiny egg cases. When they become adults, the lice are able to move onto other heads.

Head lice grip hair with their claws. They can move rapidly from hair to hair on their six legs.

Disco Snail

Some parasites only succeed in completing their life cycles by living on different organisms at different life stages. The broodsac is a parasitic flatworm that lives as a larva in a snail and as an adult in a bird, getting from one to the other because birds eat snails. More amazingly, the broodsac lures birds to the snail it is inside by making the snail's eyestalks pulsate with color—just like disco lights. The worm lives and feeds in the gut of a bird, which passes broodsac eggs in its waste. Snails grazing on grass where birds have left their droppings then eat the eggs, and the cycle begins again.

Extreme!

Brain Changer!

Broodsac larvae burrow out of a snail's gut and make for its eyestalks. There they grow bigger, feeding on the snail. They also take control of their host's brain, making it flip its personality. Before, the snail was shy and hid in the shade. Under the control of the larvae, it hangs around in the open where birds can easily spot it.

Birds that see a snail's eyestalks pulsating with color think they are caterpillars.

Tenacious Tapeworm

The tapeworm is a parasite that lives deep inside a host's intestine. It can stay there for years, slowly feeding in the dark. The usual signs that a person has a tapeworm are feelings of being full and also quite hungry—and little white pieces of worm coming out of their waste.

Host to Host

A tapeworm spends some of the early part of its life cycle as an embryo inside one host. The pork tapeworm embryo lives in a growth, called a cyst, inside a pig's muscles. If a person eats pork from that pig, the embryo may hatch inside them and then develop into an adult worm. The adult has a long, flat, white body made up of many segments. Each segment can reproduce by forming fertile eggs inside. Segments break off and are passed with the host's feces. The eggs may infect a pig if it eats soil or plants that are contaminated with human waste.

A magnified image of a tapeworm's head shows its suckers and hooks.

Extra Extreme

Tapeworms that infect humans are puny compared to their giant parasite cousins. The tapeworm that uses a sperm whale as its host can reach 100 feet (30 m) in length, made up of more than 40,000 segments.

Getting a Grip

Life inside an intestine is not easy for a tapeworm. The wall of the intestine is constantly moving, and the tube is full of soupy, half-digested food. The tapeworm has developed several processes, or adaptations, for living there. These include using strong suckers and hooks on its tiny head to grip the intestine wall so the worm does not get washed away. Instead of a mouth, the worm has skin that can easily absorb food from around its body.

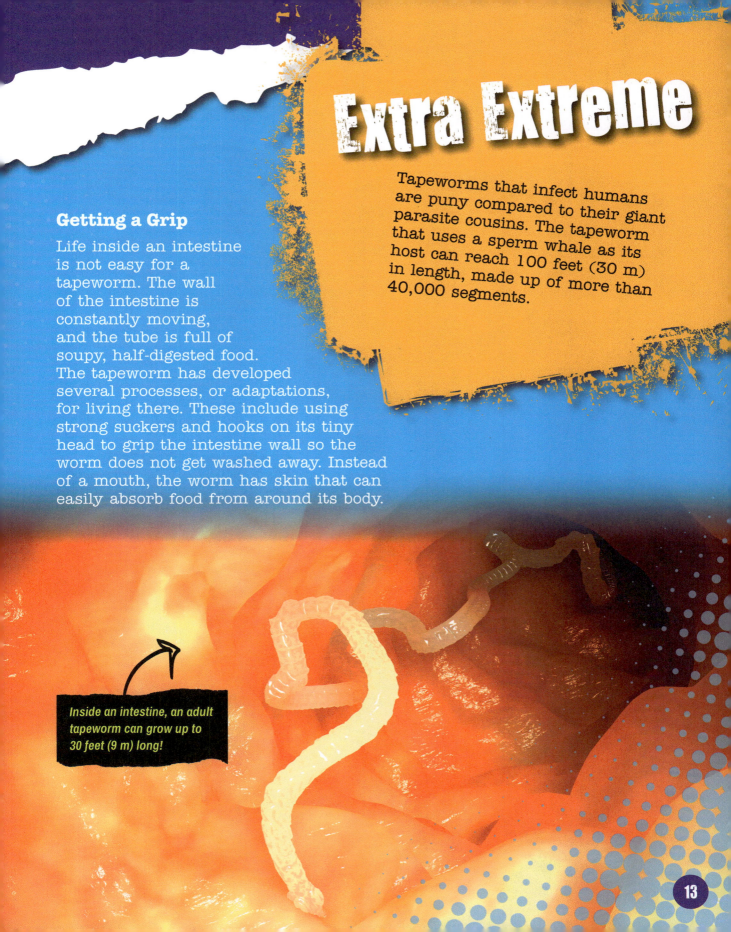

Inside an intestine, an adult tapeworm can grow up to 30 feet (9 m) long!

Killer Plasmodium

Plasmodium is a tiny parasite that causes malaria—one of the worst diseases in the world. Malaria results in anything from fever and sweats to death in millions of people. They catch the disease when they are bitten by mosquitoes that are infected with plasmodia parasites.

Vampire Insects

Female mosquitoes have a thirst for blood. They need to eat blood in order to grow and make their eggs develop as part of their own life cycle. Mosquitoes can smell a human's sweat or breath from around 100 feet (30 m) away. They fly toward the smell, land, and plunge their long mouthparts into the skin. Then they start drinking blood. As she feeds, a mosquito infected with plasmodium will inject immature forms of the parasite with her saliva.

The blood that a female mosquito steals from animals provides proteins that she needs in order to lay eggs.

Cell Demolition

The young plasmodia stream through human blood to the liver. There they change shape, multiply into thousands, and break out from the organ. They then move inside red blood cells, feed, and multiply again. There are so many plasmodia that they burst the cells open. The new organisms infect and demolish more cells, and this damage makes people sick. If an uninfected mosquito bites someone with malaria, it may eat plasmodia and then transmit the disease to other humans.

In some places, people spray chemicals to kill mosquitoes.

Extreme!

Super Sniffers

Plasmodia have an extreme trick for making sure mosquitoes bite people and pass on the parasites. They give the female mosquito a new superpower—an incredible sense of smell. Mosquitoes with plasmodia living inside them can sniff out humans three times farther than those without.

Chapter 3
Creepy Crawly Tactics

Insects are creepy crawlies with many different life cycles. Some life cycles last a few days, and others take years. Most insects start with lots of tiny eggs, which hatch into young that need a combination of luck, tactics, and skill to become adults that successfully have their own young.

Shape-Shifters

Many insects undergo big changes in shape as they grow from egg to adult. Dragonfly young are called nymphs. They live underwater, hunting insects. Then one day, they crawl up plant stems to the surface of the water. The chemicals making up their bodies slowly rearrange, and eventually their skin splits to reveal adult dragonflies. The eggs of beetles, flies, and butterflies hatch into larvae, which then change into pupae before transforming into adults. The extreme shape-shifting found in most insect life cycles is called metamorphosis.

An adult four-spotted skimmer dragonfly emerges from its brown pupa.

Butterfly Bluffers

Butterfly larvae, or caterpillars, need to eat plenty of food to get fat enough to change into pupae. A blue butterfly caterpillar avoids using its energy by bluffing red ants into feeding it. It produces a chemical that tricks the ants into thinking the caterpillar is an ant larva. Ants take the caterpillar to their nest and feed it. A caterpillar may even make noises like the queen ant to get more food than other ant larvae.

Blue butterflies smell so much like ants that ants will defend them if predators attack!

Extreme!

Ant Eaters

Some blue butterfly caterpillars cannot wait to be fed, so they help themselves to ant larvae and pupae. In this way, they can eat larger meals, become pupae more quickly, and get out of the ant nests sooner—just in case the ants see through their bluffing and decide to attack.

Flesh-Eating Wasp

Look at an ichneumon wasp and you cannot help but notice what seems to be a totally terrifying stinger. However, all is not what it seems. The stinger is actually an ovipositor, or egg-laying tube. A female wasp uses its ovipositor to allow her young to feast on living flesh.

Driller Killer

Some ichneumons seek out insect larvae living in tunnels inside fallen logs. The wasps land on the logs and scurry around, flicking the long antennae on their heads to detect smells and vibrations of feeding larvae. Once they have found the right spot, they start drilling their ovipositors into the wood toward their chosen larvae victims. A female then lays a single egg next to or on the larva. Some ichneumons look for larvae in the open. Then they plunge their ovipositors straight into them.

A female ichneumon wasp can take up to 40 minutes to drill a hole with her ovipositor.

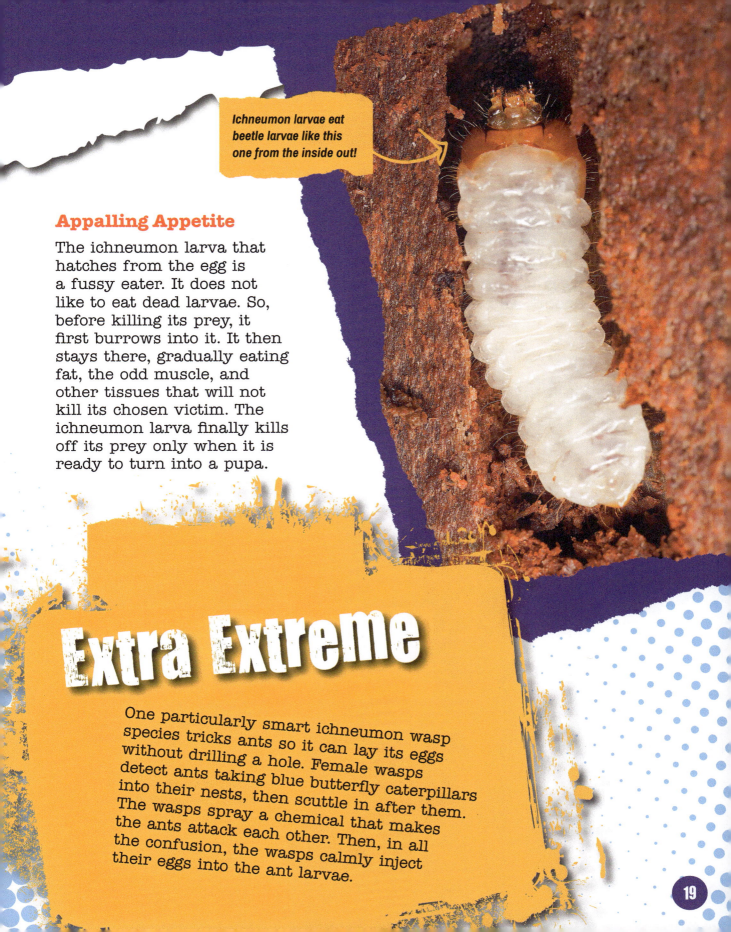

Ichneumon larvae eat beetle larvae like this one from the inside out!

Appalling Appetite

The ichneumon larva that hatches from the egg is a fussy eater. It does not like to eat dead larvae. So, before killing its prey, it first burrows into it. It then stays there, gradually eating fat, the odd muscle, and other tissues that will not kill its chosen victim. The ichneumon larva finally kills off its prey only when it is ready to turn into a pupa.

Extra Extreme

One particularly smart ichneumon wasp species tricks ants so it can lay its eggs without drilling a hole. Female wasps detect ants taking blue butterfly caterpillars into their nests, then scuttle in after them. The wasps spray a chemical that makes the ants attack each other. Then, in all the confusion, the wasps calmly inject their eggs into the ant larvae.

Easygoing Cicada

Cicadas are insects that like to take their time completing their life cycles. Some cicadas remain as nymphs underground for 17 years before burrowing out in swarms of hundreds. They then all change into adults, breed, and start the cycle again.

Growing Underground

A cicada nymph lives 1 foot (30 cm) underground, drinking sap from the roots of a tree. It is not until its 16th birthday that it digs a tunnel toward the surface. There it waits until the temperature rises. Then it emerges and starts climbing the tree trunk. After a week of feeding, it stops and sticks to the trunk. The nymph's skin splits to reveal a strange, pale, twisted creature. It bends, unfolds its wings, and darkens in color. The cicada has finally become an adult.

A cicada sheds its nymph skin and emerges as a winged adult.

Meeting Mates

Adult cicadas have one thing on their minds—breeding. Males call loudly, hour after hour, to tell females they are around. Females also call to tell males that they have heard them. Once males and females have located each other, they mate. The females then slice open twigs and lay their eggs inside. The eggs hatch into tiny nymphs that fall to the ground and start digging.

Adult cicadas have short bodies with wide-set, bulging eyes and veined wings.

Extreme!

Cicada Chorus

Cicada adults have skin that buckles inside their abdomens a bit like a crushed soda can. The rapid clicks the skin makes create a loud buzzing or sawing noise to call other cicadas. Many cicadas call at exactly the same time in chorus, making a sound so loud it can be painful for listeners, such as birds, which then decide to eat other insects instead.

Chapter 4
Smart and Deadly Swimmers

Like insects, fish lay eggs. Some fish have extreme ways of looking after these eggs to help their young survive. Others have unusual ways of finding mates and making sure they breed successfully.

Clownfish

Amazingly, all clownfish are born male—but they can change sex. The biggest, or most dominant, fish in a group grows into a female. She mates with a male clownfish and lays the eggs. When this female dies, the largest and fastest of the male clownfish does something extraordinary. It turns into a female so it can take her place! Then, it can start to breed with one of the more dominant males. The change of sex cannot be reversed.

Clownfish were named for their bold striped coloring, which looks like the face paint on a clown.

A Dangerous Home

A clownfish female lays hundreds of eggs on a rock near a sea anemone, a tube-like creature that fires poison from its tentacles. The male parent usually guards the eggs until they hatch about a week later, after which the young clownfish live among the anemone's stinging tentacles, immune to its toxins. Clownfish are safe from predators there, and they feed on the remains of fish paralyzed and eaten by the anemone. In return, the clownfish keep the anemone healthy by eating damaged tentacles and scaring off predators. They even provide nutrients in their feces for the anemone.

A female clownfish lays hundreds of eggs. All hatchlings will hide among anemone tentacles to keep safe.

Extreme!

Making Mucus

Before a young clownfish lives with an anemone, it swims around its future home, brushing parts of its body against the tentacles. The fish gets used to the stings and builds up a layer of mucus on its skin that makes it immune to the fish-eating anemone's sting.

Sea Horse

If there were awards for "best dad" in the animal kingdom, the male sea horse would be a sure winner. Sea horses are unique—male sea horses are the only male animals on Earth that get pregnant.

A Courtship Dance

When a male and female sea horse are ready to breed, they take part in daily dance routines. They intertwine their tails and swim together. Then, the dance (lasting for up to eight hours) ends with the female carefully laying her eggs inside a pouch on the male's stomach. The eggs are then fertilized in the pouch.

Experts believe that the sea horse courtship dance ensures that the female is ready to lay the eggs in the male's pouch at the same time as he is ready to fertilize them.

This male sea horse is about to give birth. The baby sea horses will live on their own after they leave the pouch.

The doting sea horse dad carries the eggs in his pouch for up to 25 days. All that time he controls how salty the water is inside his pouch, so the eggs can develop properly and the babies get used to the saltiness of the sea. The eggs hatch inside the pouch, and then the male sea horse squeezes muscles in the pouch to eject the babies out into the ocean.

Extra Extreme

A male sea horse can carry as many as 2,000 babies at a time in his stomach pouch. Sea horses produce vast numbers of young because babies are at risk from predators and starvation if they are washed away from feeding areas. In fact, fewer than five baby sea horses in every 1,000 survive to adulthood.

Sand Tiger Shark

You probably know that sharks are ruthless killers and among the ocean's most lethal predators. But did you know that baby sand tiger sharks kill and eat their own brothers and sisters inside their mother's uterus?

Killer Baby Sharks

The life cycle of the sand tiger shark has to be one of nature's most extreme—with a literal fight to the death for survival between the babies inside their mother.

A female sand tiger shark has two uteruses. After becoming pregnant, the shark will carry up to 12 baby sharks in each uterus. The pregnancy lasts approximately nine months, but around five months into that timeframe, the largest baby shark in each uterus will begin to feed on its siblings. By the end of the pregnancy, only two killer baby sharks will survive—one inside each uterus.

Fully grown sand tiger sharks are approximately 8 feet (2.5 m) long.

Sand tiger sharks are named for their habit of swimming along the ocean floor.

Extreme Survival Strategy

The killing and eating of siblings by one shark fetus may be an extreme life cycle process, but it has a purpose. It ensures that a female sand tiger shark ultimately carries and gives birth to just two live babies. Therefore, the babies that do survive are able to grow bigger than the babies of other shark species that give birth to large numbers of live young. As a result, after birth, the surviving baby sand tiger sharks are less likely to be killed and eaten by predators in the ocean.

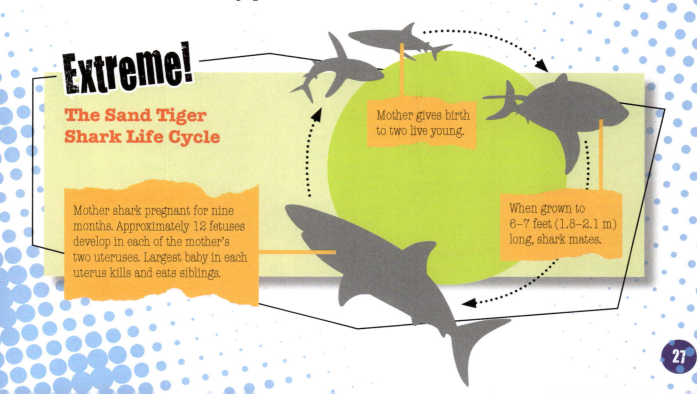

Extreme!

The Sand Tiger Shark Life Cycle

Mother shark pregnant for nine months. Approximately 12 fetuses develop in each of the mother's two uteruses. Largest baby in each uterus kills and eats siblings.

Mother gives birth to two live young.

When grown to 6–7 feet (1.8–2.1 m) long, shark mates.

Sockeye Salmon

Young sockeye salmon live in the Pacific Ocean. As they become adults, they embark on an extreme trip to the river where they were born. This is a one-way journey. After all that effort, they will breed, and then die.

Early Years

A young salmon spends its earliest years in the river where it hatched from an egg, or sometimes in a nearby lake. The salmon then swims downstream toward the ocean, where it lives for about three years, feeding on tiny sea creatures called plankton, small fish, and occasionally squid. When fully grown, the salmon joins the millions of other fish starting to migrate home. They swim up the river where they began their life cycles.

Sockeye salmon can leap 10 feet (3 m) in the air as they attempt to clear waterfalls and rapids during migration.

Turning the River Red

When it enters the river, the sockeye is a bluish color. However, as it swims upstream, it starts to change to bright red with a greenish head. These are the breeding colors. The salmon also loses weight as it burns energy swimming against increasingly fast-flowing water and dodging predators such as osprey and bears. Eventually the survivors reach the shallowest parts of the river. Females lay at least 2,000 eggs each, which the males fertilize. Then the river turns red with dead salmon.

Salmon turn red to show other salmon when they are ready to breed. Once the eggs have been laid, the males and females die within a few weeks.

Extreme!

Amazing Memories

Sockeye salmon have brains that are extremely sensitive to Earth's magnetic field. This pattern of magnetic forces is slightly different at any point on Earth. The salmon have remarkable memories—they can remember exactly what the magnetic field was like where they entered the ocean as youngsters, which allows them to return to that exact spot three years later as adults.

Chapter 5
Battles for Life

Laying eggs is a key part of the life cycle of reptiles and birds. Eggs keep the growing young safe but also provide convenient snacks for predators. So parents usually go to great lengths to protect the eggs that they lay in nests and the babies that hatch out of them.

Protective Packaging

To protect developing embryos, reptile eggs have tough rubbery skin and bird eggs have hard shells. A food store, called yolk, provides nourishment. Some babies, such as the young of snakes and the Australian brush turkey, are ready to feed on their own right after hatching. Others such as robin and hawk chicks hatch blind and featherless and would die without parents to care for them and feed them.

A baby alligator uses a special egg tooth to slice open its shell so it can start life outside the egg.

Alligator Babies

Female alligators may be fierce creatures, but they make very protective mothers! Female alligators build and lay their eggs in mounds of rotting vegetation at river edges. In the summer, the hatchlings call to tell their mom they are hatching. She then digs the nest open and helps them into the water, often by carrying them delicately in her mouth. She then stays near her young and protects them for the next two years as they feed and grow.

Extra Extreme

Whether an alligator hatches male or female comes down to one thing—temperature. Alligator nests warm up as the plants they are made from rot. Eggs in a cooler part of the nest, around 86°F (30°C), hatch as female babies, while those in a hotter part, around 93°F (34°C), become male.

Alligators are powerful, armor-plated reptiles with around 80 teeth in their long jaws.

Green Sea Turtle

Green sea turtles are reptiles with long-distance life cycles. Females swim hundreds or thousands of miles between their feeding grounds and the beaches where they lay eggs. These are the same beaches where those females started life.

Turtle Tours

Over 90 percent of a green sea turtle's life cycle is spent in the ocean, where it feeds, swims, and sleeps. Young sea turtles are carried along by ocean currents and feed on floating seaweeds. Adults spend much of their time grazing on abundant beds of sea grass. Each year, adults mate and then females migrate to particular sandy beaches to lay their eggs.

A green sea turtle digs a deep nest, then covers it with sand. The nest protects the eggs and keeps them moist and at the right temperature.

32

Just one in 1,000 green sea turtle hatchlings survives to become an adult. If it survives, the sea turtle could live for 100 years!

Night Nests

Females reach shore at night. They haul their heavy bodies, each weighing 300 pounds (140 kg) or more, up the beach and then use their front flippers to dig pits in the sand. A female then lays more than 100 eggs in the pit and covers it with sand. She may lay up to eight separate sets each nesting season. After two months, 2-inch (5-cm) long hatchlings break out of their shells and crawl as fast as they can to the sea. However, the little sea turtles are easy prey for birds and crabs, and, once in the water, they may encounter many other predators.

Extreme!

Green Gardeners

Green sea turtles are like underwater lawn mowers. When they graze on sea grasses, this action not only looks after the sea grass beds but also makes the plants grow better. Sea turtle waste helps, too, as a fertilizer. Sea grass provides food and protection for many young fish and crabs. Without it, these creatures might die.

Cuckoo

Some species of cuckoo have an extreme way of avoiding the hard work of being parents. These birds, known as brood parasites, lay their eggs in nests belonging to other birds and let the birds' parents do all the work for them.

Egg Imposters

When a female cuckoo lays a single egg inside another bird's nest, there is a risk that the other bird will spot the new egg and abandon the nest to make a new one elsewhere. To stop this from happening, the cuckoo has several tricks up its sleeve. It might throw out an egg already there, to keep the same number of eggs in the nest. Or it might lay an egg that looks just like the host's eggs, so the other bird cannot spot the difference.

A cuckoo chick often grows to be much bigger than its foster parent.

Cuckoos lay their eggs in other birds' nests and do not care for their young, which they never get to see.

Cuckoo Conqueror

The host bird incubates, or warms, the cuckoo egg and protects it along with her own eggs. However, she gets no thanks for this. After the cuckoo chick hatches from its egg, it usually throws out any remaining eggs and any other babies from the nest. Then the hungry chick mimics, or copies, the cries of the host mother's own chicks so that it gets all the food she brings back to the nest to give to the nestlings.

Extra Extreme

Some species of cuckoo migrate vast distances between breeding and feeding grounds. The yellow-billed cuckoo and black-billed cuckoo breed in North America and then fly across the Caribbean Sea to summer feeding grounds—a non-stop flight of around 2,500 miles (4,000 km).

Emperor Penguin

Emperor penguin chicks begin their life cycles inside eggs in the Antarctic—the coldest place on Earth. It is like hatching in a freezer. Only the extreme devotion of their dads gives the chicks any chance of surviving.

Icy Incubators

Emperor penguins breed in winter. The ice is most stable then, but temperatures are as low as −58°F (−50°C) and the freezing wind blows at 125 miles per hour (200 kph). The female lays a single egg on the ice and then returns to the sea. The male is left to lift that egg onto his feet and tuck it under a layer of feathered skin, known as a brood pouch. This keeps the egg warm, so the chick inside can start to grow, and allows the dad to walk around, too.

A male emperor penguin risks freezing to death to keep its egg warm on its feet at the coldest time of year.

Both parents take turns feeding their hungry chick with food that they bring up from their stomachs.

Huddle Up

Emperor penguins have thick feathers, but it is still hard to keep themselves and their eggs warm. So, even though penguins are usually quite aggressive toward each other, the males huddle together in large groups to keep warm. They even take turns being on the outside. They do this for two whole months, until the females return to help feed the chicks that are ready to hatch.

Extreme!

Near Starvation

During the two months that the male emperor penguin incubates its egg, it never feeds. The bird cannot leave the egg for even a short time to swim in the sea and catch something to eat, because the chick inside would die. So when the female returns to help feed the chick, the starving male races to the water to feed at last.

Chapter 6
Killers and Caretakers

Mammals are animals that give birth to live young that feed at first on milk from their mothers' bodies. Mammal young are also cared for by at least one of their parents during the first, vulnerable stages of their life cycles. However, some mammal life cycles are far more extreme—including that of the lion.

Family Pride

Lions live in groups called prides, with a dominant male leader. This male is also the father of every baby lion, or cub, in the pack and he protects them all. The cubs' problems begin when a male leader gets older and weaker. Then a new male from outside the pride chases off or even kills the leader and takes over the pride.

Male lions kill cubs in prides when they take over, to start their own generations of lions.

New Life

One of his first acts as new leader is to kill all the cubs by biting them on the back of their heads and necks or crushing their abdomens. This disturbing act has a very real purpose. When a new male takes over a pride, he wants to have cubs of his own. The killing of cubs results in their mothers quickly becoming fertile again and ready to have more babies. This increases the chance of the new male having offspring. Also, if the leader does not kill infant males that are not his own, those males might then kill him when they grow up.

Extra Extreme

When mothers find their dead cubs, they sometimes eat their bodies. This is hard for us to understand, but lionesses need to eat all the healthy meat they can get. If they stay strong and fit, they can protect their other living cubs and family members, too.

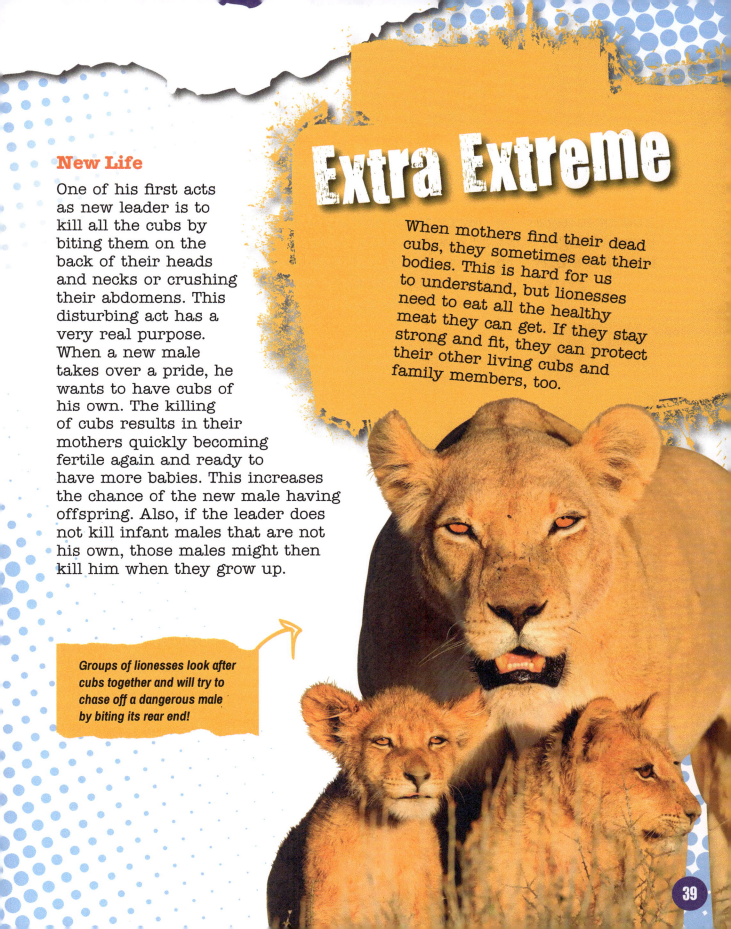

Groups of lionesses look after cubs together and will try to chase off a dangerous male by biting its rear end!

Kangaroo

Young kangaroos begin their life cycles in a very unusual way. Kangaroos are marsupials. Marsupials are mammals that give birth to very small, undeveloped young that grow inside pouches of skin on the front of their mothers' bodies.

Journey of a Jellybean

A young kangaroo, or joey, is born when it is smaller than a jellybean and weighs next to nothing. The baby is helpless at this stage. Its eyes are closed, it cannot hear, and it has no fur. Yet the joey has to leave its mother's birth canal and crawl all the way up to the pouch, using its tiny arms. It follows a path in its mother's fur that she licked with her tongue all the way to her pouch.

Joeys stay inside their mother's pouches until they look far too big to be doing so. They can leave the pouches at this stage, but soon hop back in.

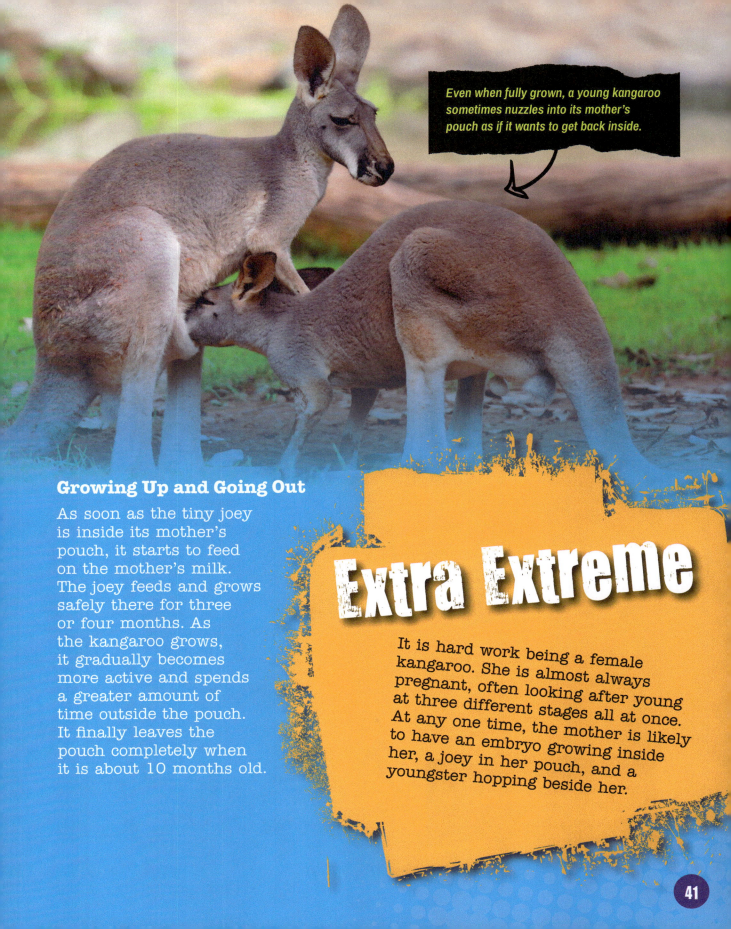

Even when fully grown, a young kangaroo sometimes nuzzles into its mother's pouch as if it wants to get back inside.

Growing Up and Going Out

As soon as the tiny joey is inside its mother's pouch, it starts to feed on the mother's milk. The joey feeds and grows safely there for three or four months. As the kangaroo grows, it gradually becomes more active and spends a greater amount of time outside the pouch. It finally leaves the pouch completely when it is about 10 months old.

Extra Extreme

It is hard work being a female kangaroo. She is almost always pregnant, often looking after young at three different stages all at once. At any one time, the mother is likely to have an embryo growing inside her, a joey in her pouch, and a youngster hopping beside her.

Wildebeest

Young wildebeests have a dramatic and terrifying start to life. As soon as they are born, they must stand on their own four, shaky feet in order to escape from some of the most ferocious predators on Earth.

Born to Run

In Africa, during February and March each year, around 500,000 calves are born to herds of wildebeests. Their mothers usually give birth standing up, and as soon as the calves hit the ground, they have to stand up and try to walk. Most manage to walk within minutes of being born and can run in less than two hours. This is a matter of life and death—the herd will not be able to help the calves if hungry lions, hyenas, or cheetahs are watching.

Young wildebeests have to be ready to run within hours of being born or they will not survive.

Young wildebeests have to keep up with the herd during migration as predators are more likely to chase them than the adults.

A Terrifying Trip

Every year, vast herds of wildebeests travel to find food over very long distances of up to 1,000 miles (1,600 km). This migration starts soon after the calves are born. So, within days, they have to be able to run fast enough to keep up with the herd, which will not stop to wait for calves that fall behind. The herd forges ahead, crossing rivers and lakes in huge numbers. Many calves are injured, lost, drowned, or killed by predators along the way.

Extreme!

Getting Lost

As soon as a calf is born, it follows its mother. If a calf gets lost and cannot find its mother, it starts to follow the closest moving thing. Usually this is another wildebeest in the herd, but some calves have been known to start following cars, people, or even predators.

Chapter 7
Completing the Life Cycle

A full life cycle is only completed if an organism survives from its first moments of life, develops into an adult, and reproduces, grows old, and dies. This is something all living things strive for and may go to extraordinary lengths to achieve. Many parents will kill or be killed in their attempts to protect young—not only their own but also those in the group.

Perfect Parents

Many animals look after their young long after the babies have been born or hatch from eggs. Female orangutans, for instance, are devoted moms. They carry their babies continuously for a year, and many youngsters keep hitching a ride for a year or more after that. Every night, the orangutan mother also makes a fresh nest from sticks and leaves where her pampered offspring can sleep.

Orangutan mothers care for their young for seven years and give birth only once every eight years.

Protecting the Young

Animals that live in groups often care for each other's young in amazing ways and will fight to the death to protect each other's babies. Protective female elephants will stampede, knock down, and crush any animal that gets too close to calves in their herd. Adult giant otters raise their bodies out of the water and screech, squeal, and snort at predators such as jaguars. The important thing for all animal families is that the young survive to continue the circle of life.

Extra Extreme

Baby meerkats need to drink their mother's milk, called suckling, for 10 weeks after they have been born. Then, life becomes more serious. Adults start to bring youngsters challenging food to experiment with, including some of Africa's most dangerous creatures, like scorpions, snakes, and spiders.

Meerkat females will even produce milk for cubs that are not their own!

Glossary

abdomen the part of the body that contains the stomach

adaptations changes in an animal that help it stay alive

antennae (singular is antenna) the long, thin body parts on an insect's head that are used to feel and touch

brood parasites birds that lay their eggs in other birds' nests

cells the microscopically small building blocks of living things

cyst a growth containing liquid

dominant more important or powerful than others in a group

embryo a young animal in early development stages before birth

feces solid animal waste

fertile able to reproduce and have young

fertilize to cause an egg, a female animal, or a plant to start producing young like itself

fungus (plural is fungi) a group of organisms that includes yeasts, mushrooms, and molds

host an animal or plant on which a parasite lives

immature at an early stage of development

immune resistant to or protected against a disease or danger

incubate to keep eggs warm until they are ready to hatch

intestine a long tube in the body where food is digested

larva (plural is larvae) a young animal, often an insect, with a different form than an adult

magnetic field the area of magnetic forces around Earth

marsupial a mammal whose babies grow in a pouch

metamorphosis a major change in the structure of an animal

migrate to move from one region, country, or habitat to another

mimic to copy the voice of another

nectar a sugary substance plants make to attract insects

nutrients the substances that nourish living things

nymphs young insects that have almost the same form as adults

organism a living thing

ovipositor the body part used to deposit eggs

pollen a fine powder produced by the male part of a flower

pollinate to move pollen from one flower to another and cause seeds to grow

pupae (singular is pupa) insects between larva and adult stages

sap a sugary liquid containing food made in a plant's leaves

species a type of living thing

spores the cells produced by fungi that can make a new fungus

suckle to drink milk from teats on a female mammal's body

toxins poisons

tuber a thick underground stem

For More Information

Books

Callery, Sean. *Life Cycles* (series includes: *Mountain, Desert, Forest, River*). New York, NY: Kingfisher, 2011–13.

Higgins, Nadia. *Life Cycles Through Infographics* (Super Science Infographics). Minneapolis, MN: Lerner Publishing Group, 2013.

Hirsch, Rebecca. *Science Lab: The Life Cycles of Plants*. Ann Arbor, MI: Cherry Lake Publishing, 2011.

Silverstein, Alvin and Virginia. *Metamorphosis: Nature's Magical Transformations*. Mineola, NY: Dover Publications, 2013.

Websites

Find out about some amazing animal life cycles at:
www.uen.org/themepark/cycles/animal.shtml

Watch and learn about great animal migrations at:
www.natgeotv.com/ca/great-migrations/videos/growing-up-butterfly

Find out more about the Atlantic salmon life cycle at:
www.nasco.int/atlanticsalmon.html

Publisher's note to educators and parents: Our editors have carefully reviewed these websites to ensure that they are suitable for students. Many websites change frequently, however, and we cannot guarantee that a site's future contents will continue to meet our high standards of quality and educational value. Be advised that students should be closely supervised whenever they access the Internet.

Index

alligators 30, 31
antennae 18
ants 8, 9, 17, 19

banksia 4, 5
brood parasites 34
broodsacs 11
butterflies 16, 17, 19

caterpillar fungi 9
caterpillars 11, 17, 19
cells 15
cicadas 20–21
clownfish 22–23
cones 4, 5
cuckoos 34–35

dragonflies 16

eggs 4, 10, 11, 12, 14, 16, 18, 19, 21, 22, 23, 24, 25, 28, 29, 30, 31, 32, 33, 34, 35, 36, 37, 44
elephants 45
embryos 12, 30, 41
emperor penguins 36–37

fertilization 4, 12, 24, 29, 39
flies 16
flowers 4, 5, 6, 7
fruit 7
fungi 8–9

giant otters 45
green sea turtles 32–33

head lice 10
hornbill birds 7

incubation 35, 36, 37
insects 6, 8, 9, 10, 14, 15, 16–21

jaguars 45

kangaroos 40–41

larvae 11, 16, 17, 18, 19
lions 38–39, 42

magnetic field 29
malaria 14, 15
marsupials 40, 41
meerkats 45
metamorphosis 16
migration 28, 32, 35, 43
mosquitoes 14, 15

nectar 5
nests 8, 9, 17, 19, 30, 31, 32, 33, 34, 35, 44
nutrients 5, 23
nymphs 16, 20, 21

orangutans 44
ovipositors 18

parasites 10–15, 34
pigs 12
plankton 28
plasmodium 14–15
pollen 6
pollination 7
pouches 24, 25, 36, 40, 41
pupae 16, 17, 19

sap 20
sea anemones 23
sea horses 24–25
seeds 4, 5, 7, 8
sockeye salmon 28–29
spores 8, 9
suckling 45

tapeworms 12–13
teats 41
tentacles 23
titan arums 6–7
tubers 7

wasps 18–19
wildebeests 42–43